SKIN, SCALES, FEATHERS, AND FUR

BY MARK J. RAUZON

To Erry Tara of Papua New Guinea

First Edition 1 2 3 4 5 6 7 8 9 10
Library of Congress Cataloging in Publication Data Rauzon, Mark J.   Skin, scales, feathers, and fur / Mark J. Rauzon.   p.   cm.
Summary: Describes how animals are protected by their skin, scales, feathers, and fur.   ISBN 0-688-10232-8.—ISBN 0-688-10233-6 (lib. bdg.)   1. Body covering (Anatomy)—Juvenile literature.   2. Skin—Juvenile literature.   [1. Body covering (Anatomy). 2. Skin. 3. Animal defenses.]   I. Title. QL941.R38 1991 596'.01858—dc20 90-49858 CIP AC

LOTHROP, LEE & SHEPARD BOOKS   NEW YORK

GREATER ONE-HORNED INDIAN RHINOCEROS ▲   ▼ SHORT-HORNED LIZARD

All animals are alike in some ways. One thing they all have is skin. It can be thick or thin, smooth or rough, bright or drab depending on the needs of the animal inside it. Some skin is covered by scales, feathers, or fur.

SNOWY EGRET

KOALA

SKIN

Skin is one of the most important parts of an animal's body. It not only protects the animal from disease and injury, it also helps control body temperature. Skin has the special sense of touch, too, which lets an animal feel pressure, pain, and changes in the temperature.

The rhinoceros has one of the toughest skins of any animal. Its stiff hide is several inches thick and is good protection against the razor-edged grasses and hot sun of its tropical home.

Frogs have very thin, moist skin. They can even breathe under water through their skin. Frogs cannot stay away from water for long. If their slimy skin dries out, they cannot breathe properly.

◀ GREATER ONE-HORNED INDIAN RHINOCEROS   ▼ PACIFIC TREE FROG

BAMBOO TOAD

Although they look like frogs, toads are different animals. They have rough, rubbery skin, so they can live in dry areas. This toad's skin blends into its surroundings so well that it is nearly invisible to its enemies.

Bright, attention-getting skin can protect animals, too. The flashiest tree frogs are poisonous. Their bright colors and bold markings warn enemies to stay away.

POISON ARROW FROG

GREAT FRIGATE BIRD

Colorful skin can also help attract mates. This male frigate bird inflates his red throat like a balloon to get the females' attention. To female frigate birds, round, red, featherless throats are very handsome!

SCALES

Scales are small, tough plates of a special skin called keratin. Fishes, reptiles, and birds all have scales.

SIAMESE FIGHTING FISH

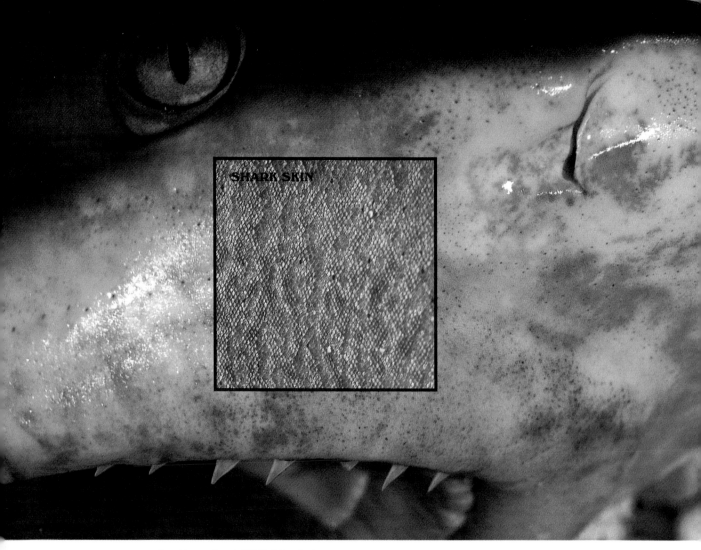

SHARK SKIN

BLACK-TIPPED REEF SHARK

Most fishes feel slippery because their scales are covered with waterproofing slime. But sharks are not slimy. Although they look smooth, they are covered by millions of tiny scales that feel as rough as sandpaper.

Many reptiles, like this snake, are covered with dry, over-lapping scales. A snake's scaly skin is shiny, not slimy.

GREEN VINE SNAKE

IGUANA

Look at all the different scales on this iguana lizard. The scales on its sides are small and flexible so it can move easily; larger, shieldlike plates protect its neck; and a row of spikes down its back make it look like a fierce dinosaur.

FEATHERS

Only birds grow feathers. Scientists think that millions of years ago birds evolved from dinosaurs and that feathers developed from scales. Birds grow scales, too, but only on their legs and feet.

PEACOCK

WESTERN GULL

Different types of feathers do different things. Short, over-lapping feathers cover a bird's body to keep it dry and warm, but long, flat feathers grow out of the wings and tail to help birds fly. Birds need to be very light to fly, so feathers weigh almost nothing.

Baby chicks are covered with millions of tiny, fluffy feathers called down that protect their skin until their adult feathers grow in. A bird's feathers fall out and are replaced with new ones throughout its life.

WHITE TERN CHICK

WESTERN GULL CHICK AND EGG

This western gull chick and egg are both speckled to help hide them on a pebbly island beach. Many baby birds have camouflaged down, but lose their protective coloring when they become adults.

Some male birds, like this peacock, grow showy feathers that help them attract mates. This peacock's shimmering tail impresses the peahens and also makes him look bigger to enemies.

PEACOCK ▶

FUR

Fur is made of millions of hairs growing very close together. Mammals are the only animals that grow hair. All mammals except dolphins and some whales grow some hair to protect their skin and better their sense of touch.

Like feathers, hair is always growing, falling out, and being replaced. Every spring, this mountain goat sheds its thick winter coat of fur, then grows it back again in the fall.

HARBOR SEALS

MOUNTAIN
GOAT

Polar bears have hollow hairs that are filled with air. The air in their fur helps keep the bears warm as they swim in the icy ocean.

POLAR BEAR

When a zebra stays still, its black-and-white striped fur looks like sunlight and shadows on tall grass. When a herd of zebras runs, the moving stripes make it hard for an enemy to single one animal out of the herd.

HORSE

Many kinds of mammals grow more than one type of hair on their bodies. This horse is covered by short, velvety fur, but it also grows long hair, called a mane, to protect its head and neck from the sun. Horses also have stiff eyelashes to keep dirt out of their eyes, and long flyswatter tails to protect their bodies against insects.

Humans are mammals, so we grow hair, too. We have manelike hair on our heads to shield us from the sun, and eyebrows and eyelashes to protect our eyes. We grow tiny hairs all over our skin except for our lips, the palms of our hands, our knuckles, our elbows, and the soles of our feet.

HUMANS

GIANT TREE FROG

TROPICAL REEF FISH

RED AND GREEN MACAW

WHITE BENGAL TIGER

Every animal has a skin to protect its body, no matter whether it is covered with scales, feathers, or fur.